What Is It?

Written by Jenny Feely

Series Consultant: Linda Hoyt

T0359885

WorldWise™
Content-based Learning

Contents

Introduction

Everywhere you look, you can see things that people have made. People make these things from different materials.

Some of these materials were first made a long time ago, and others are quite new.

Chapter 1
Made from plants

This material can be made from trees, but it can be made from other plants. It can be white, or it but can be any colour.

It can be thin enough to let light through or thick enough to let light out. It can be soft enough to wipe over your face or strong enough to hold a watermelon.

It soaks up water, but when it is coated with wax, it can hold water. It can burn, but it can be also used in the oven when food is being cooked.

It is used in packaging to stop things from breaking.

Do you know what it is?

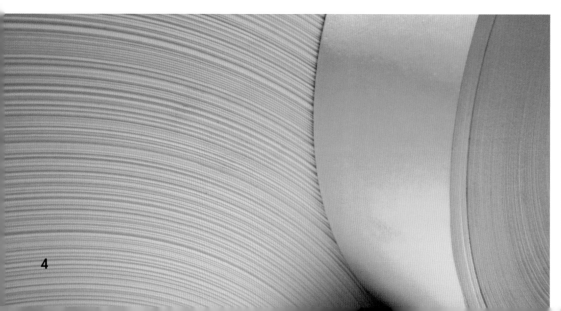

It is paper

Today, paper is most often made from trees, but it can be made from other plants.

People make paper from **wood chips** that have been crushed into a **pulp**. The pulp is rolled into sheets.

Paper is used to make books, newspapers and sheets to write on. There are many types of paper. Cardboard is made from many layers of paper stuck together.

Paper made from rice is used in cooking and can be eaten. Rice paper is sometimes wrapped around sweets.

In some countries, people use around 152 kilograms of paper each year per person. This is enough to fill a car.

Find out more

How do we recycle paper?

Chapter 2

Made from sand

People have been making this material for thousands of years. It can be many different colours or have no colour. Light can pass through it, but water and air cannot.

It can be rolled into sheets, poured into **moulds** to make different shapes or stretched into threads as thin as a hair.

It is strong and does not **rust**. Electricity cannot pass through it. It is used in telephone wires, buildings, telescopes and cameras.

Do you know what it is?

It is glass

You can see things made from glass all around you. People make glass by mixing sand with other materials and then heating them together until they melt.

Glass can be moulded into many different shapes and used to make all kinds of things that we use every day. It is strong and can be formed into thin or thick sheets.

Glass is used to make windows because it lets light through. It can be used to make jars, bottles and other containers to store things.

Glass can be recycled and reused many times.

Find out more

Glass can be added to clay to make bricks. Why do you think it is used in the brick mixture?

Chapter 3

Made from rock

It is made from a type of rock called iron ore. Iron ore is red, but this material is usually silver. It can be polished until it shines. Light, air and water cannot pass through it.

It can be made into any shape. It can be stretched into thin wires or rolled into thick, strong rope. It can be flattened into plates or moulded into strong beams.

It brings electricity to your house.

It is used to make **magnets**.

Do you know what it is?

It is steel

There are many types of steel. People make steel by heating iron ore and mixing it with other metals. Steel can be made stronger by heating and cooling it.

Steel is strong enough to make bridges and very tall buildings. But steel can also be stretched into very thin threads to make **steel wool**. This is used to polish metal and wood objects.

Steel is strong enough to keep a very thin and sharp edge without bending. This is why it is good for making knives.

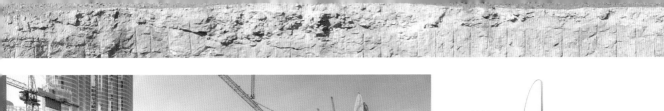

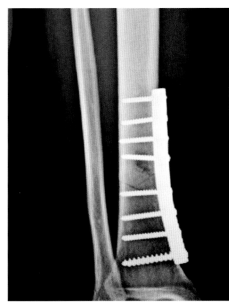

Did you know?

Doctors use steel plates and screws to fix badly broken bones.

15

Chapter 4

Made from chemicals

This material is made from **chemicals** found in oil. It can be any colour or have no colour. It can be made into any shape.

It can be flexible enough to wrap around you or strong enough to stand on. Usually, water, air or electricity cannot pass through it. It does not break easily and does not **rust** or rot.

It can be made into pipes to carry water. It can be made into threads and woven into fabric. You will find it in kitchens and gardens, and in cars and garages.

It can be hard or soft, thick or thin, coloured or see-through.

Do you know what it is?

It is plastic

People make plastic by mixing chemicals found in oil with other chemicals and then heating them. There are many different types of plastic. Electrical wires are often covered in plastic because plastic does not let electricity pass through.

Recycled plastic is used to make fence posts and furniture. Plastic can even be used to make walls that hold back the sea.

Find out more

What other things are made of plastic?

Conclusion

A wide variety of materials are used to make different things.

What materials have people used to make these things?

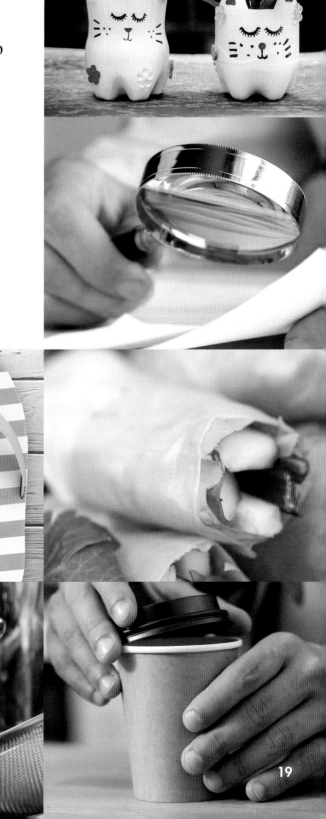

Glossary

chemicals mixtures of different types of substances, such as liquids, gases and solids

magnets metals that pull or attract certain types of metals towards themselves

moulds hollow containers used to shape melted glass

pulp soft, wet clump of plant fibres

rust a reddish substance that forms on the surface of iron when it gets wet

steel wool very fine strands of steel, twisted into a clump

wood chips small pieces of wood, made by chipping pieces off a log

Index